BLOODSUCKING LEECHES

By Tayler Cole

Gareth Stevens
PUBLISHING

Please visit our website, www.garethstevens.com. For a free color catalog of all our high-quality books, call toll free 1-800-542-2595 or fax 1-877-542-2596.

Cataloging-in-Publication Data

Cole, Tayler.
Bloodsucking leeches / by Tayler Cole.
p. cm. — (Real-Life vampires)
Includes index.
ISBN 978-1-4824-3951-9 (pbk.)
ISBN 978-1-4824-3952-6 (6-pack)
ISBN 978-1-4824-3953-3 (library binding)
1. Leeches — Juvenile literature. I. Cole, Tayler. II. Title.
QL391.A6 C65 2016
592'.66—d23

First Edition

Published in 2016 by
Gareth Stevens Publishing
111 East 14th Street, Suite 349
New York, NY 10003

Copyright © 2016 Gareth Stevens Publishing

Designer: Katelyn E. Reynolds
Editor: Kristen Nelson

Photo credits: Cover, p.1 kurt_G/Shutterstock.com; cover, pp. 1–24 (background art) happykanppy/Shutterstock.com; p. 5 Bildagentur Zoonar GmbH/Shutterstock.com; p. 7 Stephen Dalton/Minden Pictures/Getty Images; p. 9 Paza/Shutterstock.com; p. 11 Scientifica/Visuals Unlimited/Getty Images; p. 13 Dr. Robert Calentine/Visuals Unlimited/ Getty Images; p. 15 (both) Gaussianer/Wikipedia.com; p. 17 Evru/Shutterstock.com; p. 19 Maurizio Biso/Shutterstock.com; p. 21 (leech illustration) vladis.studio/Shutterstock.com.

Printed in the United States of America

CPSIA compliance information: Batch #CW16GS: For further information contact Gareth Stevens, New York, New York at 1-800-542-2595.

CONTENTS

Words in the glossary appear in **bold** type
the first time they are used in the text.

NOT JUST A WORM

Leeches are flat worms with a sucker at each end of their body. They're brown, black, or dark green. Leeches are about 0.2 to 10 inches (0.5 to 25 cm) long. There are more than 700 species, or kinds, of leeches.

Although leeches often look harmless, some kinds will suck your blood! Bloodsucking leeches have strong **jaws** and sharp teeth to bite their **victims** in order to suck their blood. These leeches are real-life **vampires**!

FACT BITE
Not every kind of leech sucks blood. Many species eat bug larvae or worms.

The smaller sucker on a leech surrounds its mouth—and that's the one it uses to suck blood!

Leech Lagoon

Leeches can be found almost anywhere on Earth. They've been discovered on every major landmass except Antarctica. Bloodsucking leeches commonly live in bodies of freshwater or on land in wet soil, but other leeches sometimes make their home in oceans.

Leeches don't like the light. They look for shallow, slow-moving bodies of water and hide underneath rocks or leaves. Like vampires, leeches are survivors. If a stream dries up, leeches simply bury themselves in the mud and **hibernate** until water returns.

FACT BITE

Bloodsucking leeches are parasites, or animals that live on or in other animals called hosts. Parasites may use their hosts for food and often harm them.

9

DINNER IS SERVED

Leeches that drink blood have a taste for a certain type of blood. Some only drink blood from vertebrates, or animals with a backbone. Some leeches only drink blood from one kind of animal, such as turtles or water birds.

When a leech bites, it drinks blood until it's full. Then it simply falls back into the water. Because their **digestion** is slow, they don't need to eat again for a few months or even up to a year!

FACT BITE

A leech can drink up to five times its own weight in blood!

Once a leech bites, the wound it creates can bleed for hours after.

9

BLOODY BITE

Leeches hunt their prey using scents or **vibrations** in the water. When they bite, leeches try to find a place their prey can't easily reach. This helps to make sure they'll have plenty of time to feed on its blood!

Many common species of bloodsucking leeches have three jaws, which cause a Y-shaped bite on the host. Matter in their spit makes it so the host can't feel what's happening. The spit also includes an **anticoagulant**.

FACT BITE

Because of the leech's spit, most people don't realize they've been bitten until they see the leech or dripping blood!

A leech uses its suckers to stick itself to its prey before taking a bite! Look at the Y-shaped bite they leave behind!

BABY BLOODSUCKING LEECHES

All leeches have both male and female **reproductive** parts, and all can lay eggs. However, a pair of leeches is needed to reproduce.

Once two leeches **mate**, the resulting eggs are laid in a jellylike cocoon, which the leech creates. The cocoon is then fixed to a rock or leaf. After several weeks, the babies come out of their eggs. Leech babies look like very small adult leeches! Leeches commonly die after laying eggs only once or twice.

Leech cocoons are full of nutrients, or the matter animals need to take in to live and grow. This image shows a leech carrying eggs.

FACT BITE

The cocoon forms a very strong, crusty skin. Studies have shown it's even able to survive being eaten by a duck!

GROSS!

People and animals can **ingest** leeches by drinking **contaminated** water. Once inside an animal's body, they feed off small **blood vessels** in the nose or throat. The animal's airways can be blocked and cause death!

One especially gross bloodsucking leech was first found in 2007. Called *Tyrannobdella rex*, the leech was named after the dinosaur *Tyrannosaurus rex* because it has a row of sharp teeth! It can stay in a person's body for weeks, sucking their blood and making them weak.

FACT BITE

If attacked, some leeches play dead to confuse their enemy!

jaw of *Tyrannobdella rex*

LONG LIVE THE LEECH

Leeches have been used for medical purposes for centuries. Leeching was very popular with ancient Egyptian doctors. The cure for many illnesses was thought to be a bloodsucking leech!

Today, doctors place leeches on areas where there's a lot of unwanted blood or swelling. Then, they just let the leeches do what they do best! The leeches' spit helps improve blood flow. Leeches are most often used on people who need small body parts reconnected to the body, such as ears and fingers.

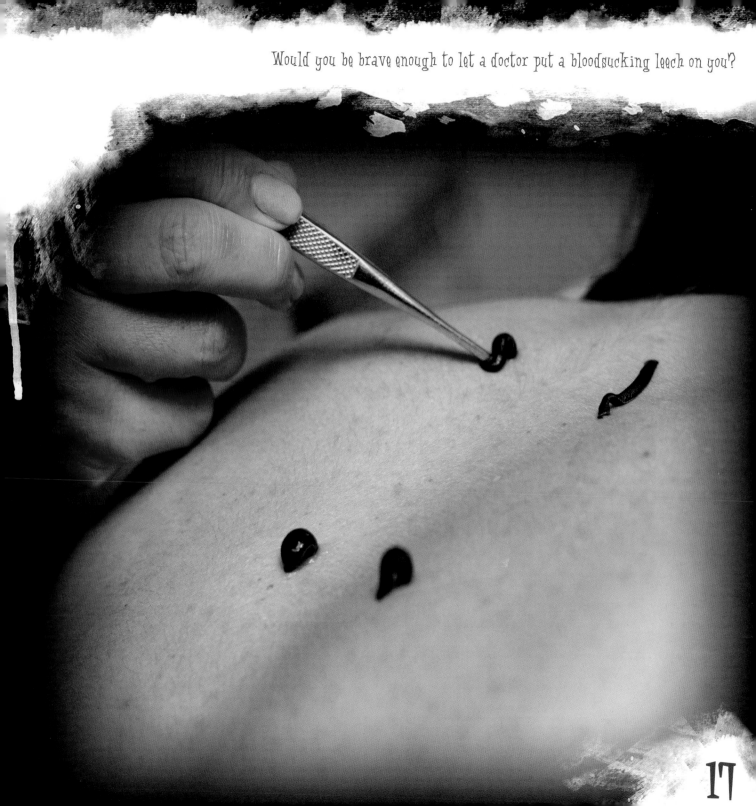

Would you be brave enough to let a doctor put a bloodsucking leech on you?

BREEDING BLOODSUCKERS

Leeches found in the wild can't be used for medical reasons on people. In the United States, only companies approved by the Food and Drug **Administration** (FDA) can sell leeches to doctors and hospitals.

These leeches come from leech farms. Leech farms **breed** leeches in large natural ponds. The leeches are cleaned and checked for sicknesses before they're sold to hospitals and doctors. There's one company in France that has been breeding leeches for more than 100 years!

FACT BITE

In Canada, leeches are considered drugs because of their spit and its ability to keep blood flowing.

BLOODSUCKERS BE GONE!

Garlic is said to keep vampires away, but how do you rid yourself of a leech? First, find the end of the leech that's stuck to you. Then gently slide your fingernail in between the leech and your skin. This will cause the leech's jaws to let go.

Once this happens, throw the leech away from you forcefully. If you don't throw it soon enough or hard enough, the leech may stick itself to your finger!

FACT BITE
Wearing bug spray before going into water where leeches may live may stop a leech from drinking your blood.

VAMPIRE VS. VAMPIRE

vampires

- bite the neck of people or animals
- have two sharp teeth
- live on land
- are often evil beings
- aren't alive

both

- drink blood
- have sharp teeth
- nocturnal
- live in dark places

leeches

- can bite anywhere on the body
- use their strong jaws and sharp teeth to bite
- commonly live in water
- don't hurt people much and can even help them
- are alive

Vampires aren't real-but they have a lot in common with leeches!

GLOSSARY

administration: a part of a government that manages the running of a certain area

anticoagulant: matter that prevents the blood from clotting

blood vessel: the tubelike pathways through which blood flows in the body

breed: to mate two animals with desired qualities in order to produce more like them

contaminated: dirty or polluted

digestion: the breakdown of food inside the body so that the body can use it

hibernate: to be in a sleeplike state for an extended period of time, usually during winter

ingest: to take food or drink into the body

jaws: the walls of the mouth

mate: to come together to produce babies

reproductive: having to do with reproduction, or an animal's creation of another creature just like itself

vampire: a made-up being who drinks human blood

vibration: a rapid movement back and forth

victim: a person or animal who's been hurt

FOR MORE INFORMATION

Books

Coleman, Miriam. *Leeches Eat Blood!* New York, NY: PowerKids Press, 2014.

Marsico, Katie. *Leeches.* New York, NY: Children's Press, 2016.

Neuman, Pearl. *Bloodsucking Leeches.* New York, NY: Bearport Publishing, 2009.

Websites

BioKIDS – Kids' Inquiry of Diverse Species: Hirudinea
biokids.umich.edu/critters/Hirudinea/
Read even more facts about leeches, their homes, and their predators.

Medicinal Leech
arkive.org/medicinal-leech/hirudo-medicinalis/image-A6403.html
Learn more about where the leeches used in hospitals come from!

INDEX